D1704035

Earnings Quality:

Spotting Earnings Manipulation

Short Selling Bad Companies!

Andrew P.C.

Contents

Introduction

These days more and more companies seem to be trying to pull the wool over investors. Maybe it starts out small, but before you know it, they are manipulating earnings right under your nose.

As a result, investors are increasingly worried about earnings quality. They begin to wonder if the company is over-earning or engaging in aggressive accounting tactics to boost stocks. The question then becomes: can the company's earnings be trusted?

I've been a student of earnings quality analysis for years. I know most of the major tricks companies use to boost profits and hide deteriorating sales performance.

Now, I'm not saying all companies engage in these practices. There are thousands and thousands of companies who don't try to manipulate earnings.

This will be a great book for investors who want to learn more about the ways earnings can be fudged to report better results. In addition, it's a great resource for investors who are looking to short bad companies.

We'll cover a variety of topics including:

*Working capital analysis to spot deteriorating trends in underlying results.

*Insider selling

*Aggressive non-GAAP reporting

*Cookie jar accounts

*Mark-to-market accounting

*Off balance-sheet accounts

*Playing with depreciation expense

*Capitalizing costs

*Internal controls

And much more!

In addition, we'll also go over a great case study to apply some of these concepts. Alright, let's get started.

Inventory

Not too many analysts look closely at the balance sheet these days. Instead, they are more focused on the income statement because that's what shows a company's revenue and profits.

More often than not, slowdown in business performance impacts the balance sheet first (through working capital) before it is finally reflected in results.

Inventory is one of the most reliable working capital metric to identify future underperformance. That's because it's hard to escape an inventory build.

If there's no demand for a company's product, inventory will build up. That's not good. <u>Eventually the bubble will burst and margins will suffer.</u> This usually takes up to 3 to 4 quarters for the catalyst to be realized.

Not enough Wall Street analysts pay attention to inventory even though they should. In fact, they rarely question the management team about it.

How To Evaluate Inventory Builds

There are a few ways to analyze inventory to determine if there is a sizable build.

The most obvious approach is to look inventory on an absolute basis. However, it should be taken with a grain of salt. Inventory could be growing 10%, but revenue could be out-pacing it at 20% growth. It doesn't look that bad then, right?

That's why a more appropriate method is to look at inventory relative to sales. If there is an inventory build, inventory should increase relative to sales.

<u>The second popular method is to calculate days sales inventory.</u>

DSI is calculated as the average inventory balance over the past two periods divided by cost of goods sold and multiplied against the number of days in the period.

$$DSI = \frac{Average\ inventory}{Cost\ of\ goods\ sold} \text{ X \# of days in the period}$$

If we're evaluating DSI on a quarterly basis, the number of days would be 90. Similarly, if the analysis was for a year, we'd use 365 days.

DSI effectively measures how long it takes the company to sell its inventory. For example, a DSI of 60 days means it takes the company (on average) 2 months to sell its inventory.

What Look For With Inventory Builds

There are many different types of inventory builds. Companies will have various explanations, which may or may not make sense. Here are some inventory red flags to watch out for:

Inventory mix

Companies typically break down inventory into three buckets: raw materials, work in progress (WIP), and finished goods (FG).

Raw materials refers to the raw inputs used to make a product. Work in progress represents inventory that is only partially completed (hence the name). Finally, finished goods represents inventory that has been fully manufactured and ready to be sold/shipped to customers.

A finished goods inventory build is typically a bad thing. This means the Company has finished goods sitting in a warehouse that it can't sell.

If finished goods increased as a percentage of total inventory, watch out. Gross margin could be hammered if the Company can't rationalize the build with strong underlying demand (i.e. sales).

Usually elevated finished goods inventory leads to inventory write-downs and/or a decline in ASPs (and hence margins).

Inventory Reserve

Companies are required to keep a reserve for potentially obsolete inventory. This is because some inventory is perishable, expires, or may otherwise become obsolete as new technology is developed.

The inventory reserve is important to pay attention to when there is an inventory build. If the Company hasn't increased the reserve, it could be in for a rude awakening.

Many inventory builds result in inventory write-offs. Basically they become useless after becoming too old. This could be a big hit to margins.

Back-end weighted guidance

By far the most common excuse companies use to rationalize an inventory build is meeting future demand. After all, if demand is about to go through the roof you should probably build up some inventory to avoid running out of stock, right?

However, that is rarely the case.

<u>Multi-period inventory builds rarely signify strong demand is around the corner. In fact, it often signifies weak demand.</u>

This is a very common excuse on conference calls. Many

companies promise analysts that demand will "pick up" in the back half of the year.

A fun analysis is to compare the revenue seasonality for this year relative to the last. Calculate how much revenue is generated in every quarter (1) on a historical basis and (2) based on sell side estimates (or the company's guidance).

If they expect a bigger percentage of revenue to be generated in the back half of the year, it should be a red flag.

More often than not, they miss guidance and will margins will be hit. Don't fall for this trick.

New products

Many companies also attribute inventory builds to new product launches. This can be true in some cases, especially if it is an important product.

The best way to test out this theory is to compare inventory trends from the Company's last big new product cycle. If inventory levels were fine then, it's probably not a new product that's the culprit.

Companies launch new products all the time and this is a very common excuse. In reality, most of the time there is just weak demand.

Weather (too hot or too cold)

Weather is always a common complaint for an inventory build.

Companies like to complain that the weather is too warm...or too cold!

When it is too cold, customers don't want to go out to retail stores. Or maybe there was too much snow and customers couldn't leave their house. Or maybe it weather delayed purchases and pushed them into the next quarter.

Most of these excuses are just bogus. I've heard them all.

There are a ton of other excuses companies use to rationalize inventory builds. Most of the time, the excuses don't hold up after you do a little digging. **Always be conscious of inventory builds because it could mean weak results are to** follow.

Accounts Receivable

Like inventory, accounts receivable is another working capital account that not enough analysts pay attention to. While not as predicative a metric as inventory, it can still be a great indicator that the business is not doing so well.

Accounts receivable is a very important revenue cycle working capital account that can signify slowing sales, credit deterioration, elevated channel inventory, and a whole host of factors.

Many short sellers use accounts receivable metrics to short stocks. Let's see why that is.

How To Measure A Receivables Build

Let's first talk about how to measure an accounts receivable build. Typically, I like to compare accounts receivable relative to revenue. If there is a build, accounts receivable should increase relative to revenue.

The other way is to calculate DSO.

DSO is calculated as average accounts receivable divided by revenue and multiplied against the number of days in the period.

$$DSO = \frac{Average \text{ receivables}}{Sales} \text{ X \# of days in the period}$$

DSO measures how long it takes the company to collect on the average receivables balance. For example, a DSO of 55 days means it takes (on average) the company 55 days to collect on its receivables.

Keep in mind that many businesses naturally have low DSOs such a retailers. This is because consumers are the end customer and pay with credit cards or cash. As a result, retailer DSOs are typically 30 days or less.

Accounts receivable analysis is best used for companies that have DSOs of at least 30 days. Anything less is just noise and will not be accurate in predicting future underperformance.

What A Receivables Build Means

A receivables build could mean a few things. The first and

most obvious is that the Company is extending payment terms to customers.

This is a frequently utilized as a tactic to drive sales.

The logic goes like this: Customers can pay in 40 days instead of the standard 30 days. This provides them (the customer) with more liquidity.

Why would a company extend payment terms to customers?

Well it could be because of increased competition or just weak demand for the product/service. The Company needs to meet numbers for the quarter, so why not extend some of the payment terms?

A big accounts receivable build could also mean the company is channel stuffing.

Think about a typical distribution channel. You have a the manufacturer, distributor (i.e. wholesaler), the retailer, and then the end customer.

Sometimes unscrupulous companies will ship more product

than is necessary to their distributor at the end of the quarter. This allows them to book sales and profits. The distributor may then return the product after the quarter.

Alternatively, the distributor could hold onto the extra inventory to sell in future periods. This means the company is effectively "pulling forward" or "stealing" sales from future periods. Obviously, this is not a sustainable strategy.

Companies will have many excuses for accounts receivable builds. In addition, there are multiple ways companies can use accounts receivable to game earnings. Let's go over what to watch out for.

Back-end weighted quarter

Check the conference call, 10Q, and press release for any mention of a "back-end weighted quarter." What the Company means a lot of sales took place during the end of the quarter (more often the last few days).

This is typically a bad thing. It can be a red flag for channel stuffing. This means the Company had to really pull in sales to meet the quarter (i.e. they "stole" sales from the next quarter).

Now, at the end of next quarter, the company needs to make up those sales that it stole by shipping even more excess product. Obviously this cycle is not sustainable and will eventually fall apart.

This is when you see a big revenue/earnings miss.

Allowance for doubtful accounts

Companies are required to keep a reserve account for receivables that could potentially be uncollectible (i.e. customers that will never pay). Basically, they have to estimate the amount of losses on receivables.

A company can use this metric to game earnings. This is called a cookie jar account because companies can use it to increase or decrease earnings.

Let's say they have a weak quarter and earnings are weaker-than-expected. Well, **the company can theoretically go in an "reverse" prior period charges (i.e. record a gain) because it believes newer customers are higher credit quality.**

To check if the company is using the allowance to game earnings, compare the allowance relative to gross accounts receivable. If there is a decline in that ratio, the company is most likely using it to boost earnings.

Aging of accounts receivable

The aging of accounts receivable should always be closely followed. This information is typically disclosed in the footnotes of 10-Q or 10-K filings.

Most disclosures will break up receivables into these categories:

Current (i.e. not past due)

<30 days past due

31 - 60 days past due

61 - 90 days past due,

And 91+ days past due

When there is a receivable build, we want to definitely check out if the aging profile of the receivables deteriorated.

If the mix shifted towards past due receivables, it could be a sign that the Company loosened credit terms. In other words, they sold product or provided services to less credit quality customers.

Customer concentration

Customer concentration refers to (1) the level of sales generated from large customers and (2) the amount of receivables due from large customers.

Companies must disclose revenue from greater than 10% customers and customers who account for more than 10% of accounts receivable in its 10-K filing.

It is often a good idea to analyze accounts receivable builds from large customers.

A big accounts receivable build from large customers could mean it provided better terms to those customers.

Watch out for big customer concentrations from companies such as Wal-Mart or Amazon. These mega companies can significantly "bully" smaller vendors into lowering price by the threat of cutting off business.

Internal controls

The 10-K must release the independent auditor's final audit opinion regarding (1) the fairness of the financials presented and (2) the effectiveness of the company's internal controls.

The opinion over internal controls refers to the Company's processes to ensure operational effectiveness and efficiency, reliable financial reporting, and compliance with internal and external laws, regulations, and policies.

In other words, internal controls refer to the processes put in place to ensure the integrity of accounting and financial information.

Most companies will receive an unqualified opinion on the audit which is also known as a clean opinion. This means the auditor believes the (1) financial statements are free of material misstatements and (2) that the internal controls are effective.

Poor internal controls can leave to multiple accounts

receivable problems including:

*double billing customers

*improper billing amounts

*billing fraud...and much more

If there is a big accounts receivable build watch out for any internal control weaknesses. Check the 10-Qs and 10-Ks to be sure.

Case Study

Alright, now that we've gone over how to evaluate inventory and accounts receivable let's take a quick look at a case study.

Our focus will be on Mattel, Inc. (MAT), the manufacturer of well-known toy brands such as Thomas, Barbie, and Hot Wheels.

Leading up to the important 2016 holiday season (Q4 2016), Mattel experienced a pretty significant surge in inventory and accounts receivable levels.

DSI had increased for six straight quarters. In addition, DSO increased for three consecutive periods.

	Q3 2016	Q2 2016	Q1 2016	Q4 2015	Q3 2015	Q2 2015
Inventory to revenue	0.507	0.932	0.803	0.294	0.486	0.864
Y/Y	4.4%	7.8%	15.7%	4.3%	18.8%	3.7%
DSI	89.6	138.2	121.7	67.3	87.0	131.9
Y/Y	3.1%	4.7%	6.3%	4.2%	10.4%	7.5%
Receivables to revenue	0.851	0.830	0.860	0.573	0.810	0.813
Y/Y	5.1%	2.1%	13.5%	4.3%	-3.1%	-1.8%
DSO	59.5	73.3	99.1	59.7	57.9	69.2
Y/Y	2.9%	6.0%	13.2%	-7.0%	-1.0%	-1.6%

Despite obvious signs of deteriorating working capital

trends, analysts were blind to the poor results that Mattel would have for the 2016 holiday season. No analysts questioned the company about the significant surge in inventory levels on the Q3 2016 conference call.

However, the company did comment on inventories briefly as shown below:

"Not surprisingly, owned inventory on our balance sheet was up year over year as we positioned the business to deliver in the fourth quarter."

As I discussed before, building inventory for demand is one of the most over-used excuses in the book. It's bogus 95% of the time.

Not surprisingly, Mattel was experiencing weak order trends from its retail customers. In addition, inventory in the channel had already begun to build significantly (as evidenced by the increase in receivables/DSOs).

Q4 2016 results were very weak. Sales declined 8.3% year-over-year to $1.83 billion, 7.6% below the average consensus expectation of $1.98 billion. Mattel also reported earnings-per-share (EPS) of $0.52, significantly worse than the expectation for $0.71.

As a result of the weak performance, shares cratered 18% the following day!

However, things were just getting worse for Mattel shareholders. Inventory and accounts receivable levels in Q4 2016 ballooned even further!

DSI increased 7.0% and DSO increased 11.0%!

As a result, investors became increasingly cautious of Mattel's inventory levels.

On the Q4 2016 conference call, Mattel did highlight higher retail inventory levels (just another word for channel inventory or the level of inventory held by retail customers).

Mattel indicated it was "working diligently" to reduce these inventory levels.

"Retail inventory was another area that was impacted by this. While a strong finish to the year helped some, our retail

inventories are moderately higher in the US and western Europe.
Fortunately, it is of good quality and composed of brands that
continue to have positive POS momentum, and we're working
diligently with our retail partners to manage it down."

However, bad results continued to plague Mattel.

Following the extremely weak 2016 holiday season, Mattel
reported weaker-than-expected Q1 2017 sales and EPS. Sales
declined 15.4% year-over-year to $735.6 million (against a
$797.6 million consensus estimate). In addition, Mattel also
reported a loss of $0.32 per-share!

<u>Shares dropped another 14% after the disastrous Q1 results!</u>

On the Q1 2017 conference call, Mattel said while it
expected results to be weak, they did not expect it to be that
weak! **However, anyone who paid close attention to the working
capital trends on the balance sheet would have been able to
easily predict the outcome that followed!**

"Going into Q1, which is a seemingly light quarter, we
expected lower revenue and gross margin because of the retail
inventory overhang coming out of the holiday period, a lighter

entertainment slate, declines in our doll portfolio, a few foreign exchange adjustments as well as some other factors. What we did not expect was a prolonged impact from the retail inventory overhang and the resulting slower pace of retail reorders."

Deferred Revenue

Deferred revenue (like accounts receivable) is an important revenue cycle working capital account. Many analysts don't follow deferred revenue closely.

However, deferred revenue deterioration could signal a slowdown or decline in revenue growth. It is also an account that is easily manipulated. In fact, many companies (particularly in the tech and software space) have used fraudulent deferred revenue to game earnings.

When Does Deferred Revenue Arise

Under U.S. Generally Accepted Accounting Principles (GAAP), revenue cannot be recognized unless (1) the product/service has been delivered to the customer and (2) collectability is reasonably assured.

Deferred revenue typically arises when customers pay in advance. Given that the good/service has not been delivered, revenue cannot be recognized.

Most deferred revenue is recognized on a straight line

basis over the contract period (like for a subscription service) or as services are performed.

What Does Deferred Revenue Deterioration Signify

As earnings quality analysts, we should always watch out for any declines in deferred revenue. If deferred revenue declined relative to revenue, more work should be done to find out why.

A decline in deferred revenue can mean a few things.

First, it can mean the company is accepting lower upfront payments for projects. This is a popular tactic to drive sales and orders in the construction, engineering, and software industries.

Here's how it works. Assume the company used to require 30% down before starting on a project. Say they changed that policy and now only require 10% down. That decline in upfront payment requirement would result in a decline in deferred revenue.

This may signal increased competition and/or weak demand.

The lower upfront payment requirement is essentially a strategy to drive sales (like extending payment terms with accounts receivable). This is a common tactic in the aerospace manufacturing industry (where prepayments can be in the hundreds of millions).

The other case is that the company may be aggressively recognizing deferred revenue. This can be due to a change in revenue recognition.

Most software companies offer hardware product bundled with software.

I won't get too deep into the accounting, but the gist of it is the amount of revenue recognized must be split between the hardware product (which is recognized upfront when delivered to the customer) and the software component (which is deferred and recognized ratably over the subscription period).

Companies can play around with that respective allocation to recognize more revenue upfront. If that happens, we would see a decline in deferred revenue.

Typically, these are very subtle changes that are not

disclosed in the 10-Q or 10-K. However, if there is a big revenue recognition change that is disclosed, you should definitely read up on it.

Other Key Deferred Revenue Concerns

In addition to lower upfront payments and aggressive revenue recognition, here are a few other areas to watch out for when analyzing deferred revenue:

Change in billing cycle:

A change in billing is usually one of the top excuses to explain a deferred revenue decline. The Company might say it went from billing annually to quarterly. This means that upfront payments might be only for 3 months instead of 12 months in advance.

An easy way to verify this is just to contact a few of the companies customers. If there was no billing change, then the excuse was bogus.

Backlog and orders:

Some companies disclose backlog metrics (it basically represents orders that are still unfulfilled). If the information is available, it would be a useful exercise to compare deferred revenue relative to backlog to assess any deterioration.

Deferred revenue in acquisitions:

When a company acquires another business, it must assign the purchase price to the net assets of the business (with any remainder plugged into the goodwill account).

If the acquired company had any deferred revenue, it must be re-valued at fair value. This requires a lot of estimation on the acquiring company's part.

One trick companies can do is to "write-up" (i.e. increase the fair value) of deferred revenue. Basically the acquirer is saying the acquiree shouldn't have recognized that revenue. As a result, this means the acquirer could potentially recognize that same revenue again (i.e. double counting revenue).

This is a rare occurrence, but it's something worth watching out for.

Non-GAAP Adjustments

Non-GAAP exclusions have become more and more prevalent the investing world.

While some companies (like Apple) don't use non-GAAP reporting it has become the exception, not the norm.

Non-GAAP Reporting just refers to metrics that do not conform to Generally Accepted Accounting Principles (GAAP). If a company reports non-GAAP results, it must be reconciled to the related GAAP metric.

The Purpose of Non-GAAP Reporting

The purpose of non-GAAP reporting is to provide investors better insight into the true earnings power of the business. After all, if there are certain unique, one-time, or unusual items, should they really be considered in the valuation of a business?

Many one-time items should in fact be excluded when evaluating a business. Some examples include:

*A big one-time lawsuit

*Negative impacts from natural disasters

*Gain from the sale of a business

More often than not, companies take advantage of non-GAAP reporting. <u>In reality, companies can exclude almost anything from non-GAAP results.</u>

These results are often not audited by a company's independent auditors and receive less SEC scrutiny than reported GAAP metrics.

As a result, investors should be made well aware of what kind of abuses can occur in non-GAAP land.

Let's go over some common non-GAAP adjustments that are completely bogus.

Stock-Based Compensation

Many companies, particularly in the tech industry, heavily incentivize employees through stock compensation. It makes sense...people tend to treat something better if they own a part of it.

Companies can provide stock compensation through a number of ways including stock options, restricted shares, and other methods.

The typical reasoning behind excluding these expenses are that they are "non-cash."

That is an absolute a bogus reason.

Stock compensation may be "non cash", but it is a real expense. <u>If the company did not pay employees high equity awards do you think they would stick around? Probably not.</u>

If the employees were not awarded high paying stock compensation, **the company would have to pay cash for them to stick around.**

Always watch out for companies that pay high levels of stock compensation. This is because if/when the stock craters, employees will have no reason to stick around.

Why stick around when the value of your stock compensation is down 30%+? This just creates a downward spiral.

Salesforce (CRM) is a prime example of stock-based compensation abuse.

Take a look at the latest earnings release where CRM reconciles GAAP operating income and non-GAAP operating income.

CRM reported a GAAP operating loss, but after excluding over $244 million in stock-based compensation, it is a "profitable" business.

| | Three Months Ended January 31, | |
	2017	2016
Non-GAAP net income		
GAAP net income (loss)	$ (51,440)	$ (25,509)
Plus:		
Amortization of purchased intangibles (a)	74,214	39,250
Amortization of acquired lease intangible	564	759
Stock-based expense (b)	244,387	158,972
Amortization of debt discount, net	6,344	6,188
Less:		
Operating lease termination resulting from purchase of 50 Fremont, net	0	0
Gain on sales of land and building improvements	0	0
Gains from acquisitions of strategic investments	0	0
Income tax effects and adjustments	(77,743)	(49,998)
Non-GAAP net income	$ 196,326	$ 129,662

Restructuring Expenses

Restructuring activities represent a broad bucket of expenses. They related to expenses incurred to "right size" the business operations.

Restructuring expenses relate to many items including:

*Employee separation costs (i.e. during layoffs)

*Plant/manufacturing closures

*Logistics and supply chain adjustments

*...and much more

I whole heatedly agree with excluding restructuring expenses from non-GAAP results...if they are unusual or non-recurring.

Many times, the companies that are excluding restructuring expenses are in perpetual "restructuring mode."

There just seems to be a restructuring every week! Are they really closing down factories and firing people every week?

Some aggressive companies may even classify normal operating expenses as "restructuring" in order to get away with excluding them through non-GAAP results.

Here's one question to ask: <u>If the company continually incurs restructuring costs (over a multi-year period) are they really "one-time" or "unusual" in nature?</u>

Most often the answer is no.

Acquisition-Related Expenses

Companies frequently exclude many acquisition-related expenses from non-GAAP results.

These expenses may include:

*Professional and advisory fees for due diligence

*Debt/interest related costs

*Costs of issuing equity

The exclusion of these expenses may be warranted if the

company made a one-time large acquisition. Many times, these expenses are incurred by roll-ups--companies who continually acquire other businesses in order to grow.

If a business continually incurs acquisition-related expenses are they really one-time in nature? Or are they just <u>normal business expenses</u> given the company's roll-up strategy?

Acquisition-Related Intangible Asset Amortization

When a company acquires another company, it must assign a "fair value" of all the net assets acquired to the purchase price.

For example, let's say company ABC acquires company XYZ for $10 million.

Company XYZ has many assets including working capital, trademarks, customer lists, intellectual property and patents, and even manufacturing equipment.

Under U.S. GAAP, companies must assign the purchase price to the fair value of the net assets.

Usually, most of the purchase price is allocated to intangible assets. This includes items such as patents, customer lists/relationships, and other intellectual property.

These intangible assets are then amortized (i.e. depreciated) over their estimated useful lives.

However, companies frequently exclude acquired intangible-asset amortization from non-GAAP results.

This dramatically overstates the earnings power of the business. **If ABC had not acquired XYZ it would have had to internally develop those intangible assets.**

By excluding acquisition-related intangible assets, ABC is basically saying there is no cost related to developing that intellectual property!

Always heavily scrutinize any non-GAAP adjustments. Companies are required to provide a reconciliation between non-GAAP results with the related GAAP metric.

A good exercise to perform is to calculate the total difference between GAAP and non-GAAP results (i.e. the "exclusions"). If the levels of exclusions has increased over the past few years, the company is likely being much more aggressive with non-GAAP reporting.

Insider Selling

Insider selling is a widely studied area. After all, a company's insiders should have the most up-to-date information about operations, right?

Insider selling can often be a precursor to stock price underperformance. That's why it's a big focus to many top short sellers in the business.

Can insider selling be used as a barometer to identify future stock price underperformance? Well...it depends. I have personally looked over thousands and thousands of Form 4s to verify this thesis.

Analyzing insider selling is both an art and a science. Most insider sales data is just noise. However, there are subtle nuances to identify future stock price underperformance through these sales.

Who are "insiders?"

Insiders are the top executives of a company. This includes the C-suite (i.e. CEO, CFO, COO, etc.) and potentially employees on the vice president level. It also includes the board of directors.

How do you find a particular company's insiders? They will be disclosed in the proxy statement (Form DEF-14A filed with the SEC).

Every proxy statement will disclose the beneficial ownership of the company's most important insiders. Beneficial ownership just refers to the number of shares each insider owns.

Why Follow Insiders?

The stock purchases and sales of insiders should be followed closely because they are the people managing the business.

They have the most up-to-date information about sales, profits, strategy, and much more. If they don't like what they see, insiders are allowed to sell shares (often with far less limitations than the public is aware of).

This can be a red flag for investors.

Why would anyone want to invest in a business where the management team is selling shares? There have been numerous academic studies that have identified insider selling as a potential indicator of stock price underperformance.

Let's see how we can spot the red flags of insider selling.

Why Do Insiders Sell Shares?

Analyzing insider sales should be more than just looking at a particular series of transactions and extrapolating a conclusion.

After all, insiders sell shares for a variety of reasons. In fact, there's a Wall Street saying that goes something like this:

People sell shares for many reasons, but they only buy for one reason (they expect the stock price to increase).

Here are a few legitimate reasons why insiders would sell shares:

*Diversify the portfolio: Insiders are just like normal people managing their net worth. Part of building a strong portfolio is diversification. Insiders already generate a substantial salary/bonus from the company. On top of that, they typically receive equity awards. It's not unreasonable to assume that they want to diversify their net worth into other investments.

*To make a big purchase: Sometimes insiders need to sell shares to make purchases. They typically have a vast portion of their net worth invested in the business. What happens when they need to buy a house? They would probably need to sell some shares.

*Need liquidity: Sometimes insiders just need liquidity. The easiest way to achieve that is to sell their stock holdings. Maybe they need to pay out money in a divorce or invest in a startup.

When Does Insider Selling Signify Underperformance?

Insider selling should not be analyzed by itself. It's difficult to make the argument for future stock price underperformance by just looking at the stock transactions of the VP of Sales.

Insider selling analysis must be combined with other factors in a holistic approach.

<u>Here are a few factors that strengthen the case for underperformance:</u>

*Group selling: Wolves move in packs. If multiple insiders are selling a material portion of their beneficial ownership that should be taken as a red flag. The more insiders that are selling shares, the stronger the correlation.

What is deemed "material"? Well in my experience, anything over 10% of an insider's beneficial ownership is material. Typically, bad insiders like to move together. If there is a significant level of insider selling by many c-suite executives, something may be amiss.

*Earnings reports: Some executives may sell several months before an earnings report. The cause might be because sales/profits have lagged guidance and/or sell-side estimates. After the company reports weaker-than-expected earnings, the stock craters. Check to see if any insiders have done this in the past.

*Sales relative to prior years: Many insiders have 10b5-1 stock plans. These types of plans were originally envisioned for founders (i.e. Bill Gates) to sell their significant ownership stakes.

Under a 10b5-1 plan, insiders can sell a predetermined number of shares over a predetermined time period. If the current year insider selling is high (across all or a portion of insiders), it may be a red flag for stock price underperformance.

*Past history: One factor that is often overlooked is an insider's track record with selling shares. We want to focus on insiders who have historically avoided big losses by selling their shares ahead of time.

To do this, pull up the history of the insider's stock sales over a minimum of three years. See how the stock price performed subsequent to the sale on a 3 month, 6 month, and 12 month basis. Then, compare those losses relative to the S&P 500 or some other index.

If the executive seems to have an "innate ability" to trade

his/her own shares, it might be something worth looking into.

*Executive departures: What's one reason why executives jump ship? Well, the most obvious is things aren't going so well. If you see any significant insider selling combined with mass executive departures, something might be wrong with the company.

Deterioration in results: Some insiders like to sell shares when the business begins to 'crack'. This can be due to a slowdown in revenue growth, margin weakness, working capital deterioration, cash flow weakness, or a variety of other factors. Pay attention to insider selling when results are not good.

Insider Selling Case Study

Let's look at a case study of Hanger, Inc. to see how insider selling can be a big red flag. Hanger is the largest provider of orthotic and prosthetic services in the U.S.

In early 2014, several of Hanger's insiders had sold stock. <u>The list included:</u>

*VP Chief Information Officer Walter A. Meffert, Jr.

*CFO George E. McHenry, Jr.

*Director Eric Green

*President-Linkia, LLC Rebecca Hast

*EVP Richmond L. Taylor

*CEO Vinit K. Asar

*Chairman Thomas P. Cooper

*EVP Kenneth Wilson

Many of these insiders sold a huge chunk of their beneficial ownership...including CFO George E. McHenry (who sold over 29,000 shares or over 60% of his beneficial ownership).

What is even more interesting is that during this period, Hanger announced that (1) George McHenry would retire as CFO at the end of the year (12/31/14) and (2) Richmond Taylor would also retire at the end of the year.

In the case of Hanger, we have (1) material insider sales by executives and (2) mass executive departures. In addition, Hanger had experienced ballooning accounts receivables from poor credit practices. They also had bloated inventory levels that were obviously overstated.

In August of 2014, Hanger reported weaker-than-expected results and reduced guidance. The stock cratered from the low $30s to the low $20s.

Even after that the bad results, Hanger reported a string of bad news which included: (1) multiple delays of financial filings, (2) credit problems with their bankers, (3) potential fraud...and much more! The stock was ultimately delisted to the

OTC markets and it even hit as low as $2!

While the case with Hanger is on the extreme end, it serves as a cautionary tale: be careful of insider selling.

Risk Factors

The risk factors section of the 10-K is important because it basically describes everything that could go wrong with the company.

Many investors skip through this section for good reason (it's very boring to read). However, it is one of the most important sections of the 10-K.

Risk factors are often drafted by lawyers. As a result, the language can be very boilerplate (meaning it may contain very standard language).

For example, it is very common place to see things like: "if the economy weakens, demand for our products may also be weak."

Obviously, if the economy weakens, business should be impacted! That's not what we're looking for.

How To Read The 10-K Risk Factors Section

The risk factors section can contain just about anything.

As a result, keep your eyes peeled for anything that looks unusual.

One thing to read for is any changes in the risk factors section from the prior year. <u>We are looking for important (and sometimes subtle) key word changes in disclosures.</u>

These changes can just be a simple word or a phrase that could indicate business has deteriorated.

To conduct this technique, I would highly recommend reading the current year 10-K side-by-side with the prior year 10-K. This allows you to compare everything word-for-ford.

Having read hundreds and thousands of 10-Ks over the years, I have compiled a list of key factors you should watch out for:

*Changes in competition: Companies often list competitors in the risk factors section. It is a good idea to see if any new names pop up. This may signal increased competition.

*Customer concentration: Any customer that accounts for a significant percentage of sales could be a big risk. I use 10%+ as a threshold. Check to see if any customers are becoming a greater percentage of revenue. This could be a big risk as it gives that customer more pricing power.

*New/pending regulation: Any disclosures on new regulations that may impact the business should be read closely.

*Any important lawsuits: If the company is involved in a high-profile lawsuit, the risk factors section should be read to assess the potential risk.

*Commentary about debt levels: If the company is highly levered, anything discussing debt levels in the risk factors should be read.

*Dependence on certain products: Some companies generate a substantial portion of sales from one product (like Apple's iPhone). Any disclosures regarding dependence on a few key products should be closely read.

*Dependence on certain suppliers or manufacturers: Some companies rely on a few suppliers. This can be a big risk if the suppliers want to raise prices or if they go out of business.

This is by no means a comprehensive list, but it's a great

checklist to keep in mind when you're reading through the risk factors.

   Reading through this section of the 10-K is always informative. You never know what information you'll come across. One tip is to break up the reading with several breaks. The risk factors section is extremely dry reading material. You'll want to be very alert when reading these notes.

Cookie Jar Accounts

There are many cookie jar accounts a company can use to game earnings. Under U.S. GAAP, companies are required to make a variety of assumptions for certain expenses. <u>Anytime there is a high degree of management discretion regarding estimates, earnings manipulation can take place.</u>

Cookie jar accounts are accounts that companies use to "smooth over earnings".

Let's go through an example. All companies have an allowance for doubtful accounts.

Basically it's an estimate as to how much of outstanding receivables will never be paid from delinquent customers.

When a company is having a better-than-expected quarter (in terms of profits), they can increase the allowance for doubtful accounts to increase their expense (and thus reduce earnings).

Now why might a company want to report lower profits? That sounds counterintuitive.

Well maybe the company knows next quarter will be a little more difficult because a few customers already canceled orders. In that case, it makes sense to increase the reserve this quarter (when results are good), so they have a "cookie jar" to manipulate next quarters' earnings, which are not expected to be as good.

When next quarter rolls around, the company will drop the level of the reserve (i.e. reverse out previously recognized expenses) so that profits are higher.

Through this tactic, companies can "smooth out" or manipulate earnings. Always be skeptical of earnings quality when these cookie jar or reserve accounts are declining.

Here is a list of some of the most common cookie jar accounts:

*Allowance for doubtful accounts (which we already discussed)

*Inventory obsolescence: Companies are required to reserve for any inventory that might not be sold due to a variety of factors such as product expiration, technological obsolescence, markdown risk, fashion risk, etc.

*Restructuring reserve: Sometimes companies go through restructuring plans. This may involve laying off employees, consolidating production facilities, or a number of other strategic initiatives.

Let's say the company is laying off employees and it has to estimate employee severances. Well, it can "over-estimate" them this quarter to create the reserve, which can be used to smooth out earnings in other quarters.

*Warranty reserve: Many companies provide warranties on their products. As a result, they are required to estimate the cost of providing services under these warranties at the time the product is sold.

*Sales Returns: Virtually all companies experience sales returns for one reason or another. Companies are required to estimate sales returns when a product/service is delivered. This can be used to game earnings by over-estimating returns in a one period and then reversing it in another period.

This is not a full list by any degree, but it is a good

place to start when you're evaluating earnings quality.

Off Balance-Sheet Accounts

Companies can have many different off-balance sheet accounts. There are too many to name from special purpose entities who do business with the company (but are frauds) to off-balance sheet debt.

Those are a lot less common these days. However, let's go over two very common off-balance sheet accounts that should always be analyzed: (1) operating leases and (2) inventory purchase commitments.

I won't bore you with the very minute details, but there are basically two main types of leases under US GAAP accounting: capital leases and operating leases.

Capital leases are put on the balance sheet (as a debt liability) and the related asset is depreciated on the income statement.

Meanwhile, operating leases are not put on the balance sheet. Instead, they are put "off the books" and the periodic rental expense (i.e. for a building or a piece of equipment, etc) is recognized on the income statement.

Now, companies generally prefer operating leases because it is not put as "debt" on the books like a capital lease. Capital leases can increase a company's balance sheet debt levels and scare off some investors.

Always pay attention to any material off-balance sheet operating leases. We can check out the amount of operating leases that are "off balance sheet" by taking a look at the 10-K. There is a section in every 10-K called "Commitments and Contingencies".

In this section, they disclose any important contingencies and commitments they have to pay over the next few years. Let's take a look at Starbucks's commitments table (shown below):

Contractual Obligations [1]	Total		Payments Due by Period							
			Less than 1 Year		1 - 3 Years		3 - 5 Years		More than 5 Years	
Operating lease obligations [2]	$	7,285.0	$	1,125.1	$	1,902.6	$	1,561.8	$	2,695.5
Financing lease obligations		62.0		4.3		8.6		8.4		40.7
Debt obligations										
Principal payments		3,600.0		400.0		350.0		750.0		2,100.0
Interest payments		932.2		94.2		181.3		163.0		493.7
Purchase obligations [3]		1,223.1		786.4		371.5		57.5		7.7
Other obligations [4]		182.7		18.2		35.7		16.5		112.3
Total	$	13,285.0	$	2,428.2	$	2,849.7	$	2,557.2	$	5,449.9

As you can see, Starbucks has nearly $7.3 billion operating lease obligations! That's almost as much as the amount of liabilities on the balance sheet at the end of October 2016 ($8.4 billion).

Another key off-balance sheet item to watch out for is inventory purchase commitments. Sometimes companies commit to buying inventory ahead of time in order to ensure supply, secure pricing, or maybe it's just an industry standard.

If the company you are analyzing is experiencing a balance sheet inventory build, a year-over-year increase in inventory purchase commitments is not going to help.

Now, companies may say the purchase commitments are cancellable. Don't be fooled by that language. **Most companies would not jeopardize important supplier relationships by canceling important inventory purchases.**

Mark To Market Accounting

Mark to market accounting manipulation isn't as prevalent as it used to be. However, it is still worth a brief discussion. This type of earnings manipulation was made famous by the collapse of Enron in the early 2000's.

Basically, under U.S. GAAP, some assets can be reflected at fair value instead of historical cost. **Some of these types of assets include derivative securities and trading securities (i.e. equity or stocks or other types of investments).**

At the end of every period, these assets/liabilities must be "marked to market." In other words, the company must re-estimate their fair values and record a gain or loss on the income statement. Always be skeptical of any large and unusual gains that appear due to mark to market accounting.

These days, companies are required to disclose a fair amount of information about the fair value of various assets and liabilities on their balance sheet. Be sure to read these disclosures for anything that may be important.

Depreciation

Property plans and equipment (PP&E) can be a ripe area for earnings manipulation and most analysts don't track it closely enough.

Most long term assets are depreciated over their useful lives. **However, companies can play around with the useful life to reduce the periodic depreciation expense.**

The formula to calculate depreciation on a depreciable asset is: (cost - residual value) / useful life

Companies can manipulate earnings by playing with two things in the equation: (1) residual value and the (2) average useful life.

Residual value just refers to the value of the asset after the end of its useful life. It's basically what the company thinks they can sell it for. <u>Companies can decrease the periodic depreciation expense of an asset by increasing the residual value.</u>

For example, the company could say at the end of the 5 year

useful life this asset will now have a residual value of $500 instead of the prior assumption of $200. This will effectively reduce the annual depreciation figure.

Most companies will never disclose anything about their residual values. However, if you see anything buried in the footnotes of the 10-K, it should be something to watch out for. If the increase is material (i.e. important enough to earnings) than it should be reported to investors.

Similarly, companies can decrease depreciation by increasing the useful life of assets. Don't be fooled by these tactics.

Most companies provide a useful life range for different categories of PP&E.

The easiest way to determine if there was an increase in useful life is to check the useful life ranges disclosed from the current year and compare it to the prior year. However, the company could still increase the useful life of PP&E, but just within the stated ranges.

What you want to do is actually calculate an estimated

average useful life for all PP&E.

The formula to calculate the estimated useful life is:
(Average gross PP&E) / Annual depreciation expense

By "average gross PP&E", I mean the average of PPE using the beginning of the period and the end of the period.

This will effectively calculate the average useful life for all assets. If it increased, the company could be trying to game earnings.

When using this metric always be aware of the mix of PP&E. Some categories like buildings will have a useful life of a few decades (I.e. 30+) in comparison to computers (which generally have a useful life of less than 5 - 6 years).

If there is a mix shift towards asset categories that have higher useful lives, then the increase may be justified (due to simple mathematics).

Capitalized Costs

Under U.S. Generally Accepted Accounting Principles (GAAP), companies are allowed to capitalize certain costs. By "capitalize", I mean they are not put on the income statement right away as an expense.

Instead, they are put on the balance sheet and "depreciated" just like property, plant, and equipment.

The company must have some justification for capitalizing costs. For example, they must provide future economic benefits.

Let's talk about two common types of capitalized costs: (1) marketing and solicitation costs and (2) internally developed software costs.

Let's say a company is developing software to use internally (i.e. not selling it). Well under U.S. GAAP, all internal software development costs prior to "technological feasibility" are expensed (put on the income statement), while costs after "technological feasibility" has been reached are capitalized.

I won't get into the details of how "technological feasibility" is defined, but it is very subjective. <u>As a result, a company can (and is sometimes) incentivized to "reach" technological feasibility earlier in order to capitalize the costs so they are not reported on the income statement.</u>

If this happens, look for any capitalized software development costs on the balance sheet. They could be increasing at a very fast pace. Obviously it is not a sustainable benefit to earnings.

Let's take a look at another case study to look at marketing and solicitation costs. Ever hear of Restoration Hardware (ticker symbol: RH).

They are a very fast growing high-end furniture retailer. Anyways, Restoration Hardware sends out beautifully made "source books" to potential customers all across the country.

It's basically a giant magazine showcasing their products. These things can be really big--I'm talking about 300+ pages and 3+ pounds.

Well, Restoration Hardware actually capitalizes these costs

instead of expensing them. Take a look at the disclosure about their catalog source books from the latest 10-K:

"Capitalized catalog costs consist primarily of third-party incremental direct costs to prepare, print and distribute Source Books. Such costs are capitalized and amortized over their expected period of future benefit. Such amortization is based upon the ratio of actual revenues to the total of actual and estimated future revenues on an individual Source Book basis."

If these capitalized costs were to balloon, one should be very curious if they are aggressively capitalizing costs to report better earnings--in other words, they might be capitalizing costs they shouldn't be!

In the latest year, Restoration Hardware's capitalized catalog costs capitalized on the balance sheet increased by 71%!

I'll let you be the judge as to whether that is "normal."

	January 28, 2017	January 30, 2016
Capitalized catalog costs	$ 61,258	$ 35,836
Vendor deposits	13,276	22,959
Federal tax receivable	13,124	—
Prepaid expense and other current assets	29,504	20,225
Total prepaid expense and other current assets	$ 117,162	$ 79,020

Internal Controls

Every company's 10-K must disclose the independent auditor's audit opinion regarding (1) the fairness of the financials presented and (2) the effectiveness of the company's internal controls.

Fairness of the financials presented refers to whether or not they are presented without any significant mistakes and errors and in accordance with U.S. Generally Accepted Accounting Principles (GAAP).

The opinion over internal controls refers to the company's processes to ensure operational effectiveness and efficiency, reliable financial reporting, and compliance with internal and external laws, regulations, and policies.

In other words, internal controls refers to the processes put in place to ensure the integrity of accounting and financial information presented and the application of various rules and regulation.

Most companies will receive an "unqualified opinion" on the audit, which is also known as a 'clean opinion'. This means the auditor believes the (1) financial statements are free of material misstatements and (2) that the internal controls are effective.

If an opinion other than an unqualified opinion is given, it would be taken as a red flag. Sometimes it is because the company has poor controls over its accounting and finance processes. This may result in improperly reported numbers or in the worst case financial fraud.

If there is some kind of internal control weakness, the auditors must disclose what they are.

<u>**Internal control weaknesses due to anything related to revenue recognition, expense recognition, or working capital is always a red flag.**</u>

Internal control weakness generally increase the risk of fraud, improper accounting, and/or accounting restatements/errors exponentially.

Always keep a look out for internal controls when you are shorting stocks. If you're going long, be sure the control weaknesses are not glaring before making an investment.

Friday Night Dump Reporting

Sometimes companies like to bury bad news by selectively reporting information when they knew investors are less likely to pay attention.

<u>This includes releasing information:</u>

*Friday after the market closes (i.e. when people are gone for the weekend)

*Reporting information after the market close before three-day weekend (i.e. Memorial Day, Labor Day, etc).

*Disclosing key information before important national holidays Christmas Eve or Thanksgiving Eve.

So why do companies do this? It's because they think they can get away with disclosing information on days when they think no one is paying attention.

Plus, even if the news is bad, if the market has 3 days to digest the information. As a result, the impact on the stock price might be less than if it was released during the trading session.

Conclusion

Analyzing and uncovering earnings quality is both a science and an art. It is a skill that vastly improves the more you use it.

Most companies follow the same pattern of earnings manipulation. After you see them once or twice in action, you'll be able to spot them much easier.

Don't let these companies fool you by sugar coating results. Never let management paint the picture for you. Always be ready to really dig into the footnotes and see how things are running for yourself.

You'll save yourself a bunch of headaches (and money) by avoiding bad companies to invest in (or perhaps profit on such opportunities by shorting these companies).

Hopefully this book was helpful in understanding the art of evaluating earnings quality. Go out there and let these companies know they can't pull the wool over you!

If you enjoyed this book, please consider leaving a review.

I take all feedback seriously and it helps me to continue to produce great content for others.

Also, if you want to better understand how to read financial statements and SEC filings, be sure to check out my **Financial Statement Analysis** book.

You'll learn how to read footnotes, unheard of public filings, and evaluate financials to really get a competitive advantage.

These are just some of the skills you'll learn:

*The mechanics of financial statements (balance sheets, income statements, and statements of cash flows).

*Key financial ratios to evaluate profitability, returns, leverage, and efficiency.

*Valuation methodologies to assess how cheap or expensive stocks are.

*How to read key SEC filings (10-K, 10-Q, 8-K, Proxy Statements, Form 4s, etc.)

*Understand key performance indicators (same store sales, organic growth, backlog/orders, etc.)

*Learn how to dig through filings to get key information and get that extra edge!

<u>Click here</u> to get my Financial Statement Analysis book now!

Financial
Statement Analysis
The Blueprint For Financial Success

Andrew P.C.

Printed in France by Amazon
Brétigny-sur-Orge, FR

16209103R00048